A Seed for Sid

by Jenna Walton
illustrated by Melissa Iwai

 HOUGHTON MIFFLIN   BOSTON

Printed in China

ISBN-13: 978-0-547-02765-4
ISBN-10: 0-547-02765-6

4 5 6 7 8 9 0940 15 14 13 12 11 10

seed

Sid found a seed.
The seed was hard
and smooth.
Sid wanted the
seed to grow.

dirt

hole

Sid dug a hole.
He put the seed
in the hole.
Then he put dirt
on top of the seed.

3

sun

Sid waited and watched.
The sun came out
to warm the ground.

4

rain

Sid waited and watched.
The rain came down
to make the ground wet.

sprout

Sid waited and watched.
Then one day he saw
a small green sprout.

Sid waited and watched.
The green sprout
grew and grew.

vine

flower

Soon the plant was
a very long vine
with big yellow flowers.

Sid looked and looked.
The plant was too big
to be a bean plant.
It was too small
to be an apple tree.

pumpkin

Then one day Sid looked
at the plant.
What a surprise!
A big pumpkin grew
from his small seed.

10

Responding

Story Structure

Who is this story about? Where does the story happen? What happens in the story? Make a chart.

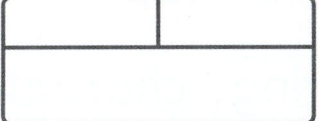

✏ Write About It

Text to World Think of a plant. Draw two pictures that show how the plant grows. Write a sentence to tell about each picture.

11

better	**thought**
night	**told**
pretty	**turned**
saw	**window**

✔ **TARGET SKILL** **Story Structure**

Tell the setting, character, and events in a story.

✔ **TARGET STRATEGY** **Analyze/Evaluate**

Tell how you feel about the text, and why.

GENRE A **fantasy** is a story that could not happen in real life.